basix B™

Syncopation
for drums

MW00522715

CONTENTS

Alfred 𝄞

Cover photo courtesy of Yamaha Corporation of America

FOREWORD

In every band or ensemble, the drummer is called upon to give that group a solid rhythmic foundation. Therefore it is important that every drummer have excellent music reading skills. The goal of this book is to first introduce basic music reading skills and then to explore many of the most common syncopation rhythms found in today's music.

Here are some suggestions on how to practice the rhythms and exercises found in this book:

1. Count out loud. This is a "must" in order to become a good reader.

2. Practice at various tempos from slow to fast.

3. Work on incorporating the syncopated rhythms you learn in this book around the full drumset (toms, cymbals, hi-hat, etc.).

4. Devote some of your practice time to playing with a metronome.

Remember, there is no substitute for a good teacher.

Below is a review of the theory you need to know in order to use this book.

GETTING ACQUAINTED WITH MUSIC

The Staff (Stave)
The drum to be played is determined by the note's position on a graph made of five horizontal lines and the spaces in between, called the staff.

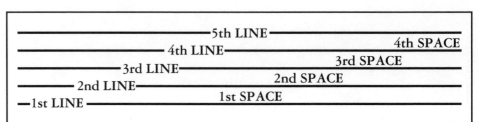

Measures (Bars) and Bar Lines
Music is also divided into equal parts, called MEASURES. One measure is divided from another by a BAR LINE. Examples end with a DOUBLE BAR LINE.

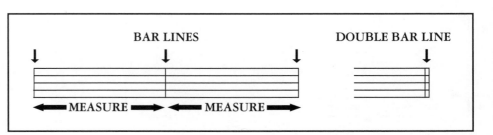

Clefs
Music for percussion is written using the percussion clef. The two vertical lines of the percussion clef extend from the 2nd line to the 4th line.

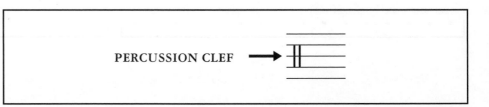

The Drums on the Staff
The BASS DRUM (kick) is notated stems down on the first space. The SNARE DRUM is on the third space.

Time Signatures
Each piece of music has two numbers at its beginning called a time signature. These numbers tell us how to count time for that particular piece.

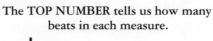

The TOP NUMBER tells us how many beats in each measure.

The BOTTOM NUMBER tells us what kind of note gets one count. 4/4 time is frequently used in the rock, blues and jazz idioms.

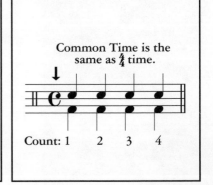

Common Time is the same as 4/4 time.

Count: 1   2   3   4

SOUND OFF:
HOW TO COUNT TIME

Notes:

𝅝	whole note (semibreve)
𝅗𝅥	half note (minim)
♩	quarter note (crotchet)
♪	eighth note (quaver)
𝅘𝅥𝅯	sixteenth note (semiquaver)

Rests:

In music, a rest is a measured silence.

▬	whole rest (semibreve rest)
▬	half rest (minim rest)
𝄽	quarter rest (crotchet rest)
𝄾	eighth rest (quaver rest)
𝄿	sixteenth rest (semiquaver rest)

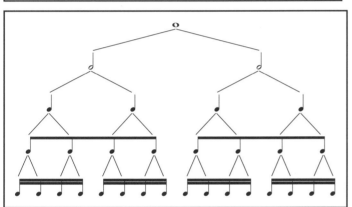

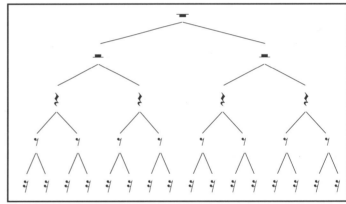

Chad Smith

Chad Smith, *the solid, powerful drummer for the Red Hot Chili Peppers, deftly combines the drive of rock drumming with the more syncopated, flowing groove of funk. He has helped turn on a generation of alternative rockers to the energy and sophistication of R&B-oriented music.*

Photo: © Lissa Wales

CHAPTER 1: Note Reading

Lesson One

Playing quarter notes, quarter rests and half rests.

16-Bar Exercise   Track 2

Lesson Two  Track 3

Playing quarter notes, quarter rests and half rests in unison.

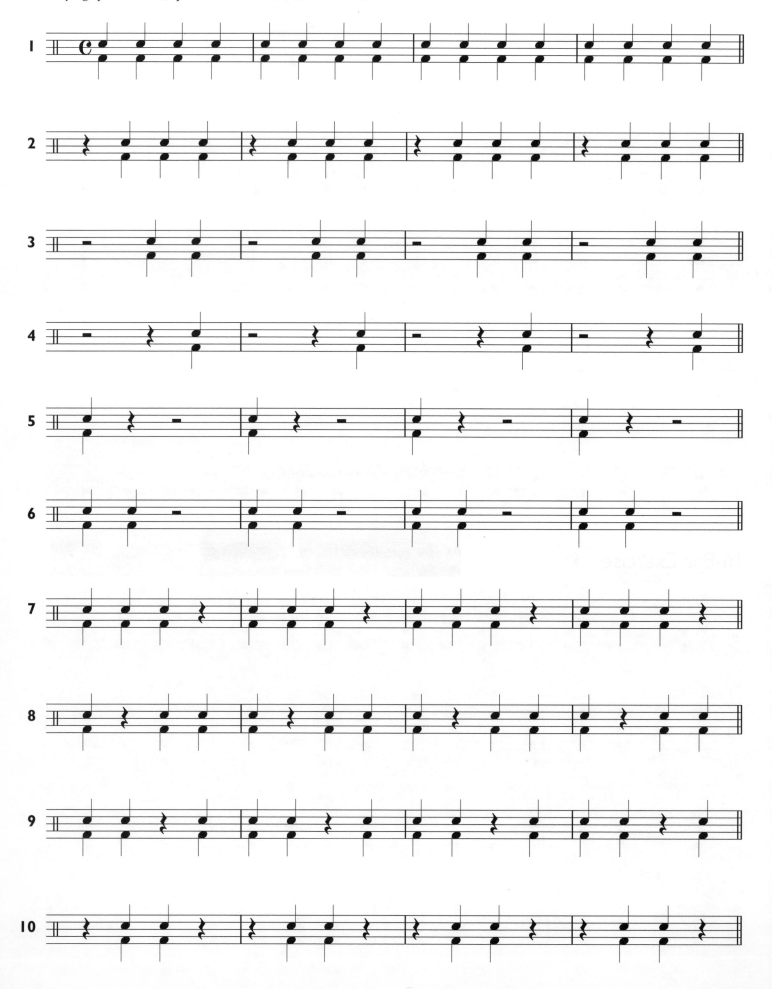

Neil Peart

As drummer for the Canadian trio Rush, **Neil Peart** helped introduce sophisticated drumming, including the use of odd time signatures and elegant solo work, to a generation of rock fans. Since the 1970s, he's been one of the most inspiring and imitated drummers in any style of music.

Photo: © Lissa Wales

16-Bar Exercise Track 4

Lesson Three  Track 5

Playing quarter notes, quarter rests and half rests independently.

Simon Phillips

British drummer **Simon Phillips** has performed with
many musical legends, including Jeff Beck and The Who.
Phillips, an energetic virtuoso, is known for a powerful-
but-precise style that incorporates, among other
elements, brilliant use of double bass-drum technique.

Photo: © Lissa Wales

16-Bar Exercise Track 6

Lesson Four

Track 7

Playing eighth notes and quarter notes.

20-BAR EXERCISE Track 8

Lesson Five

Playing dotted eighth/sixteenth notes
and quarter notes.

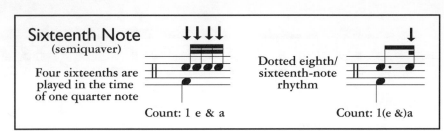

20-Bar Exercise Track 10

Introducing Triplets

A triplet is a group of three notes of equal value, usually played in the place of one note. A triplet will have the numeral "3" placed above or beneath the center note. You can remember the sound of eighth-note triplets by saying the words "mer-ri-ly, mer-ri-ly." Each word sounds like an eighth-note triplet.

Example:

Lesson Six

Playing eighth-note triplets and quarter notes.

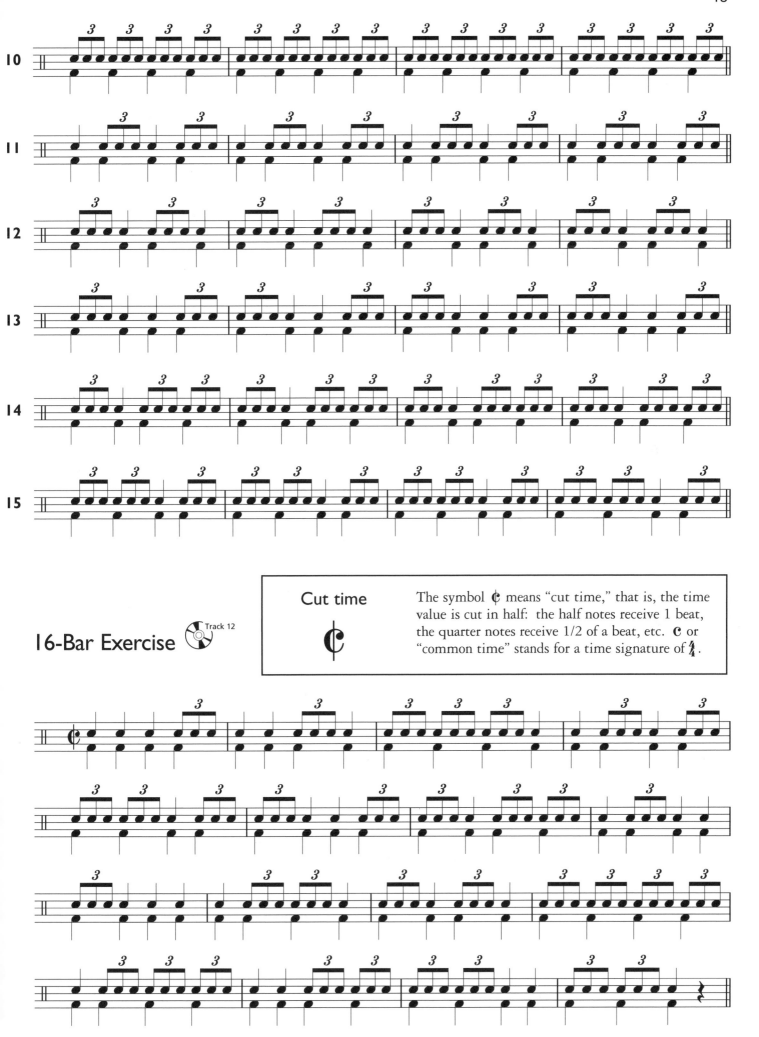

16-Bar Exercise Track 12

Cut time

𝄵

The symbol 𝄵 means "cut time," that is, the time value is cut in half: the half notes receive 1 beat, the quarter notes receive 1/2 of a beat, etc. 𝄴 or "common time" stands for a time signature of 4/4.

Lesson Seven Track 13

Playing eighth-note triplets, eighth notes and quarter notes.

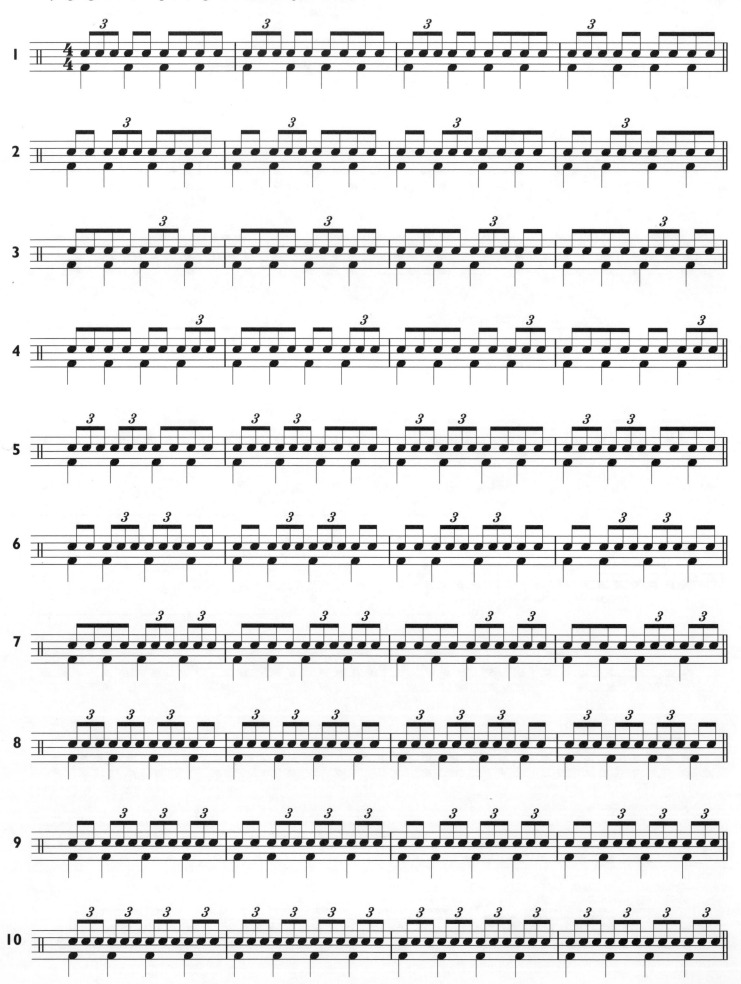

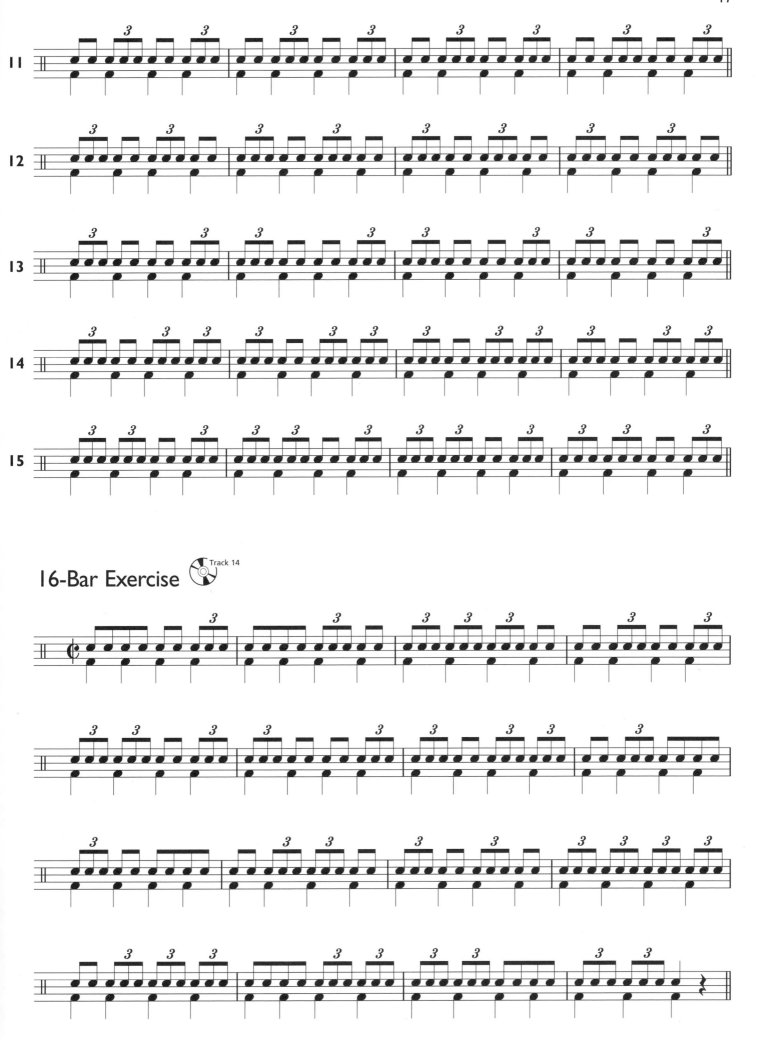

16-Bar Exercise — Track 14

Lesson Eight

Playing eighth-note triplets and dotted eighth/sixteenth notes.

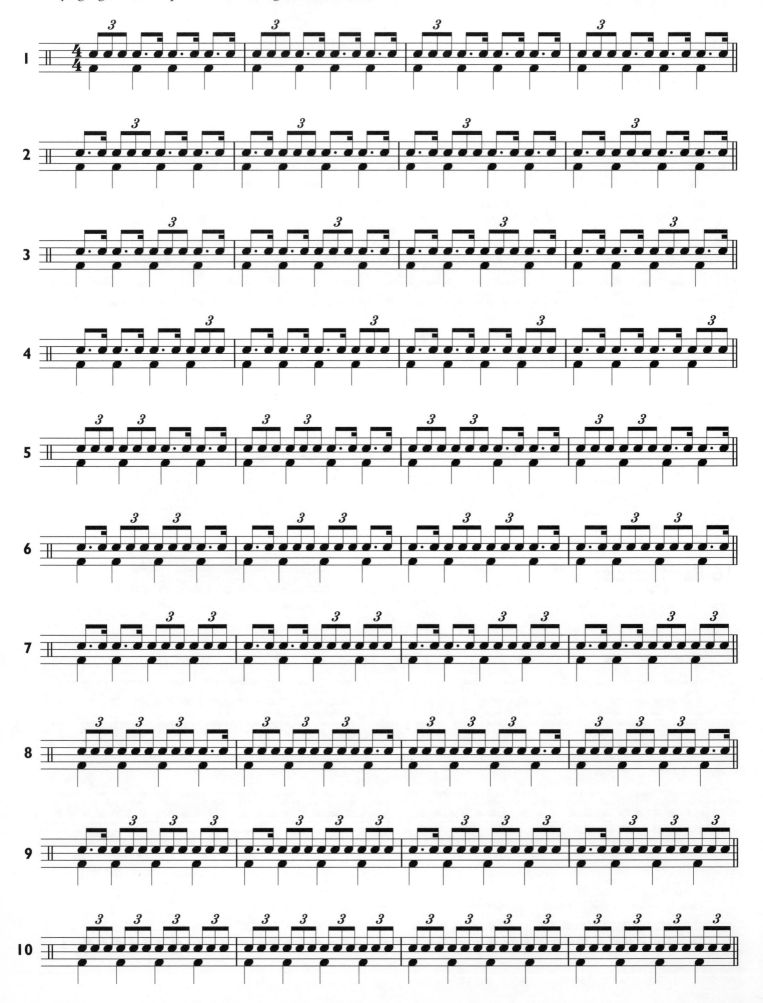

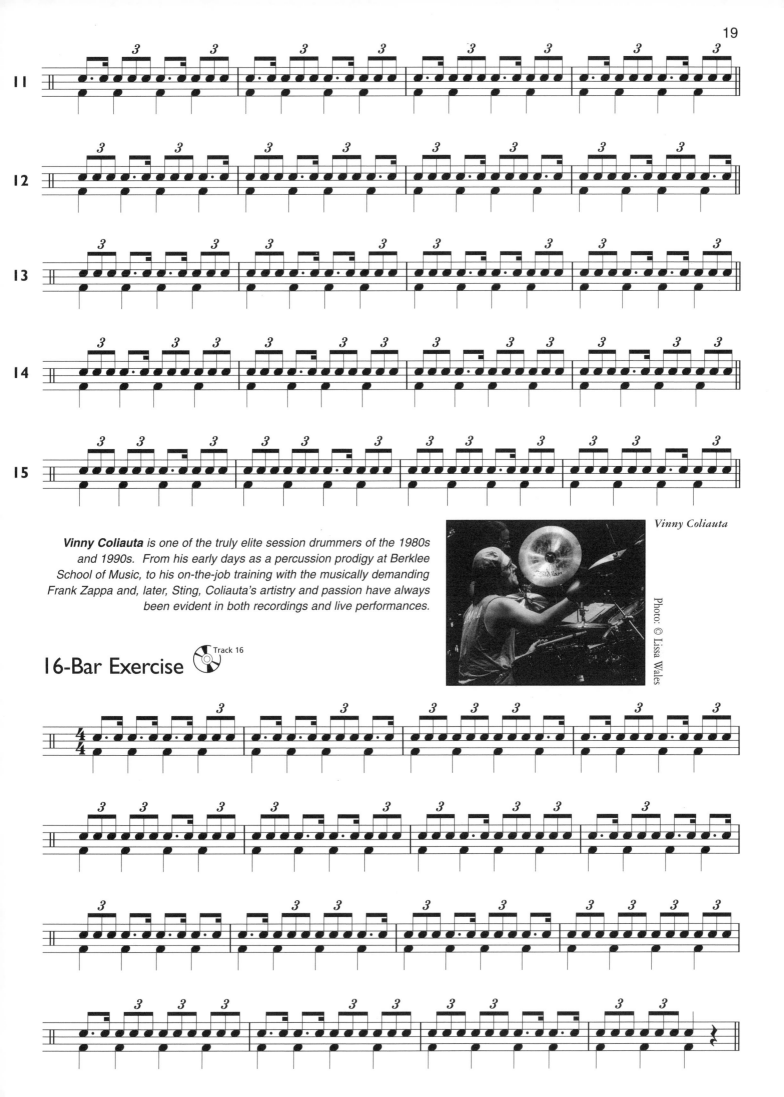

Vinny Coliauta

Vinny Coliauta *is one of the truly elite session drummers of the 1980s and 1990s. From his early days as a percussion prodigy at Berklee School of Music, to his on-the-job training with the musically demanding Frank Zappa and, later, Sting, Coliauta's artistry and passion have always been evident in both recordings and live performances.*

Photo: © Lissa Wales

16-Bar Exercise

Track 16

Lesson Nine  Track 17

Playing sixteenth notes and quarter notes.

20-Bar Exercise Track 18

Lesson Ten

Track 19

Playing sixteenth notes and eighth notes.

20-Bar Exercise Track 20

Lesson Eleven

Playing sixteenth notes and eighth notes.

19

20

21

22

23

24

25

26

27

40-Bar Exercise  Track 23

48-Bar Exercise

Track 24

| ♪ | **Eighth Rest** (quaver rest) | This symbol stands for 1/2 beat of silence. You can think of it as an unplayed eighth note. |

Lesson Twelve

Track 25

Playing eighth notes, eighth rests and quarter notes.

48-Bar Exercise

Track 26

Stewart Copeland

Photo: © Lissa Wales

One of the most important drummers to bridge the gap between several styles of music is former Police drummer **Stewart Copeland**. He has developed a widely admired and copied style that combines the best elements of rock, jazz and reggae. His influence can be heard in bands throughout the world.

Dave Weckl

Dave Weckl is considered a master of modern jazz drumming. While he has worked with many top musicians, it is his work with Chick Corea that has most contributed to his acclaimed reputation. Weckl's tremendous use of syncopated polyrhythms made him the ultimate fusion drummer.

Photo: © Lissa Wales

CHAPTER 2: Syncopation

Syncopation Set 1 Track 27

Syncopation occurs when a temporary displacement of the regular metrical accent occurs, causing the emphasis to shift from a strong accent to a weak accent.

In the examples below, each pattern (A, B and C) sounds the same, yet is written differently.

Syncopation Set 2  Track 28

The following 48 exercises begin with the 12 rhythms
found in Set 1 with new rhythms gradually introduced.

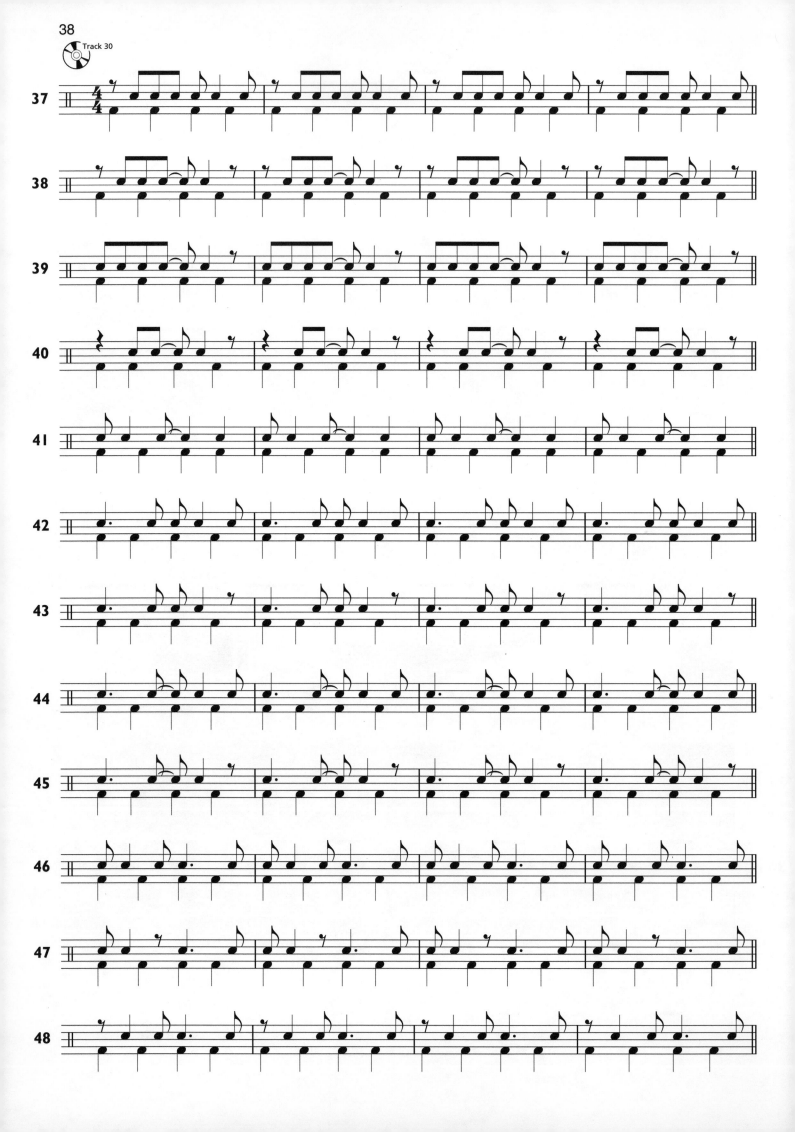

Photo: © Lissa Wales

Buddy Rich *was a masterful performer. His feel for big-band swing, which incorporated syncopated rhythms, kept him at the forefront of jazz drumming for seven decades, and earned him one of the most familiar names in modern percussion.*

Exercise One

Track 31

Exercise Two

Exercise Three

Exercise Four

Track 34

Exercise Five

Track 35

Exercise Six

Exercise Seven Track 37

Exercise Eight

Exercise Nine Track 39

> **Accents**
>
> Play accented notes (those marked with a >)
> a little louder than unmarked notes.

Elvin Jones *came into prominence as John Coltrane's drummer in 1960. It was during this collaboration with the jazz saxophone great that Jones developed his revolutionary use of non-linear ride-cymbal patterns and syncopated polyrhythms. His style set new standards for drummers world-wide.*

Elvin Jones

Photo: © Lissa Wales

Lesson One
Accented eighth notes

Track 40

For variety, the *accented notes* on pages 50–64 may be played on the small tom-tom, large tom-tom, cymbals, etc. They may also be used for accented roll studies by buzzing each note. For example:

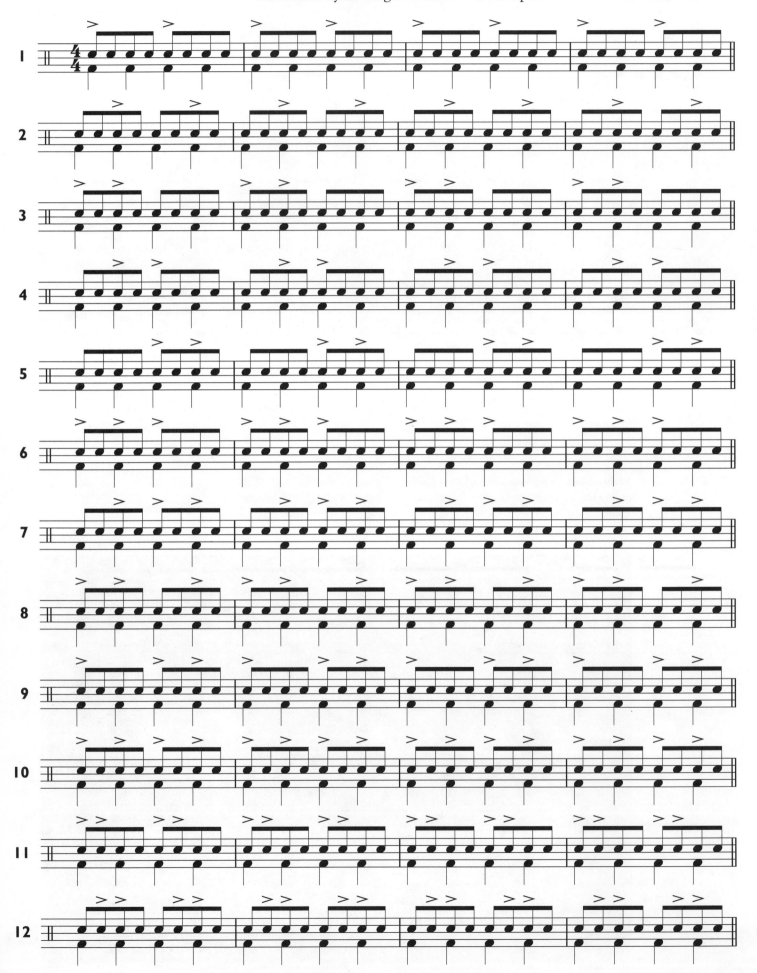

Track 41

25

26

27

28

28-Bar Exercise

Track 42

Lesson Two

Accented dotted-eighth/sixteenth notes.

28-Bar Exercise Track 45

Lesson Three

Accented eighth-note triplets

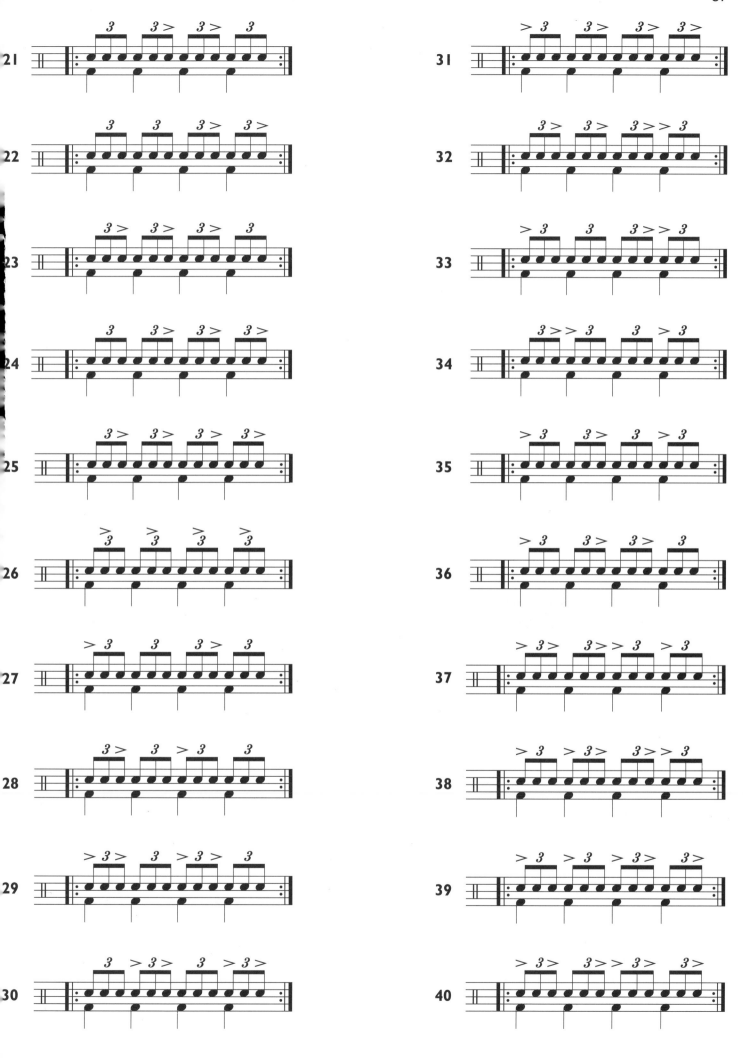

36-Bar Exercise

Track 48

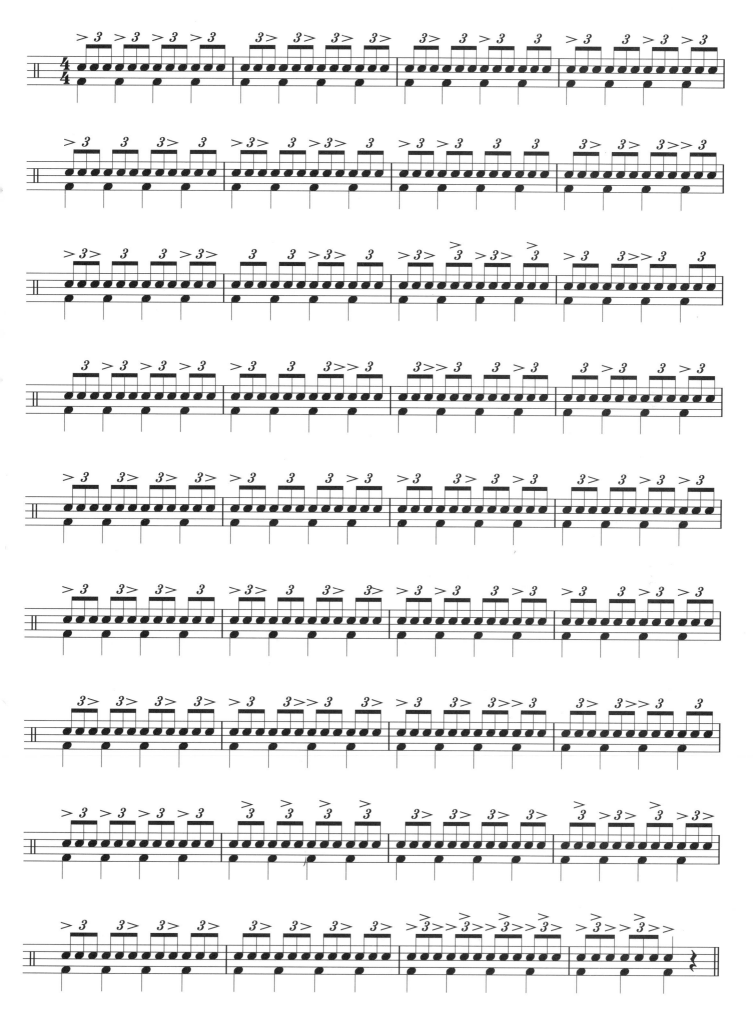

Lesson Four

Track 49

Triplets with mixed sticking

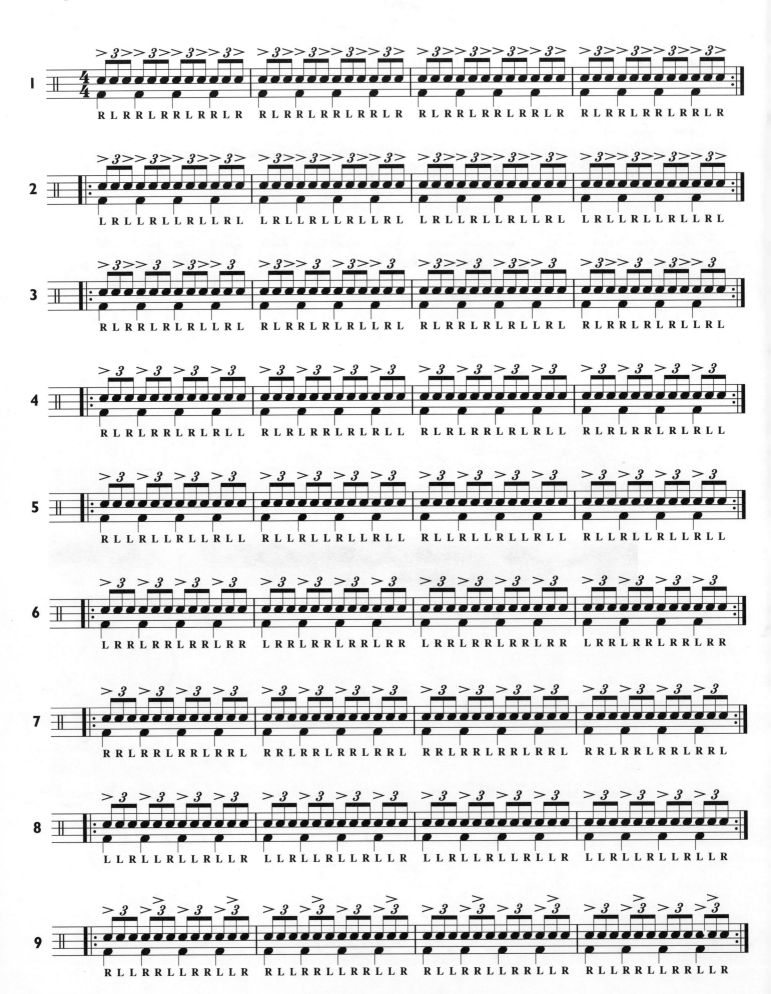

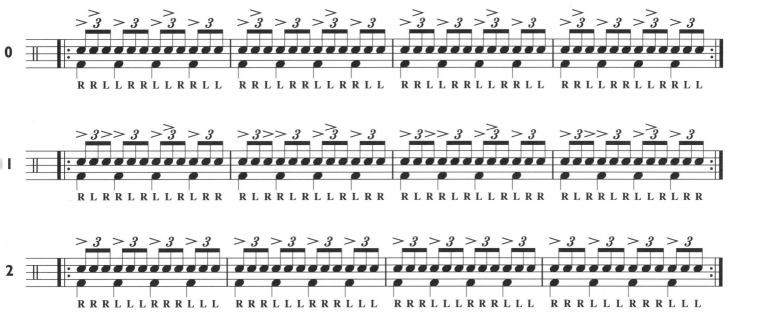

Steve Gadd

*Since the 1970s, **Steve Gadd** has maintained his reputation as one of the busiest and most versatile studio drummers working. Having recorded with Paul Simon and Steely Dan (among others), Gadd became popular in part because of his ability to apply varied percussion styles, including his tasteful use of syncopated Latin rhythms, to popular music.*

Lesson Five

Accented sixteenth notes

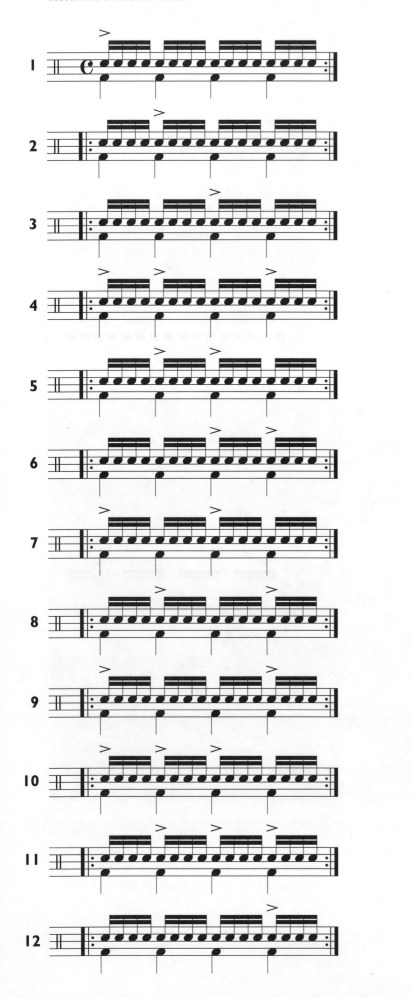

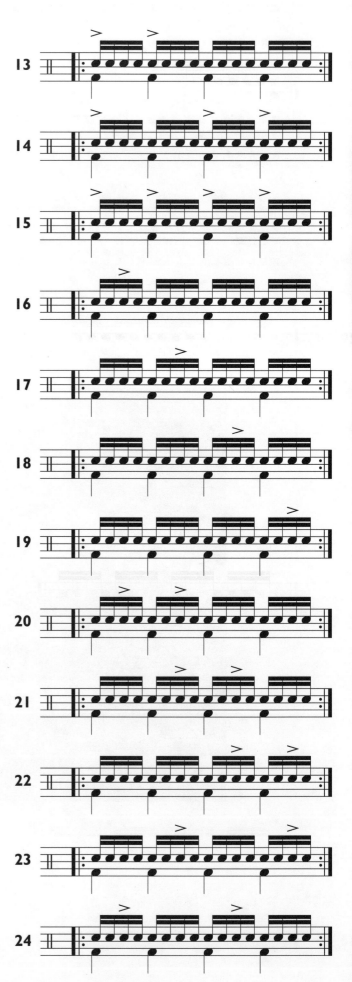

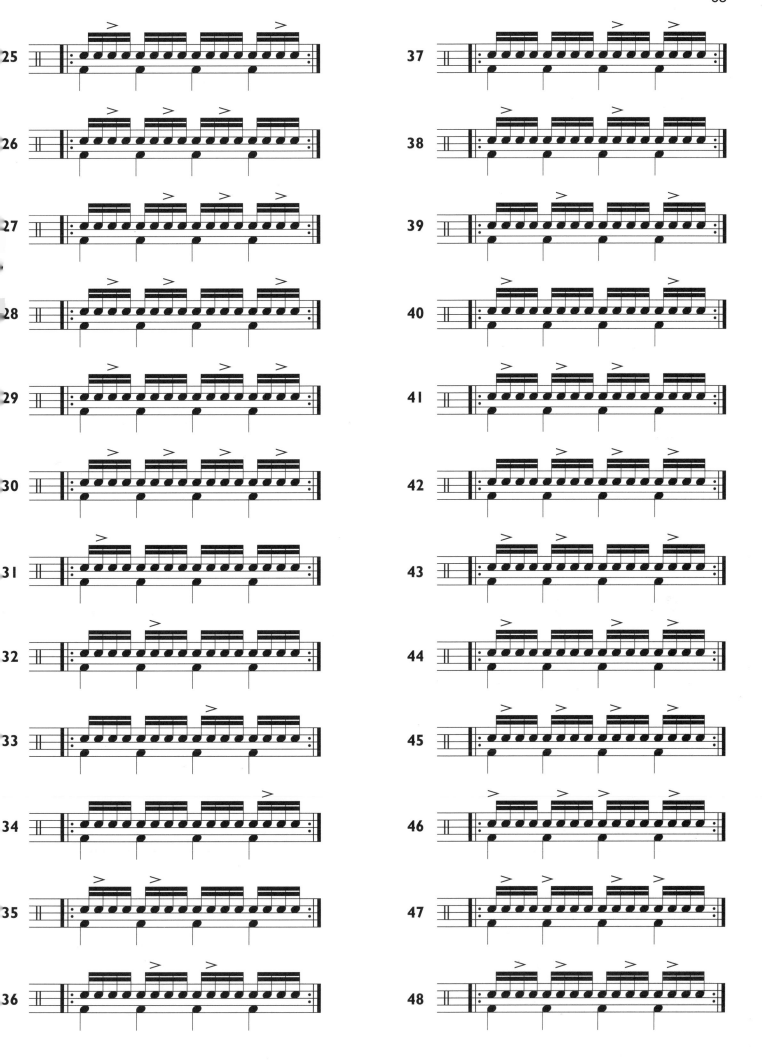

64

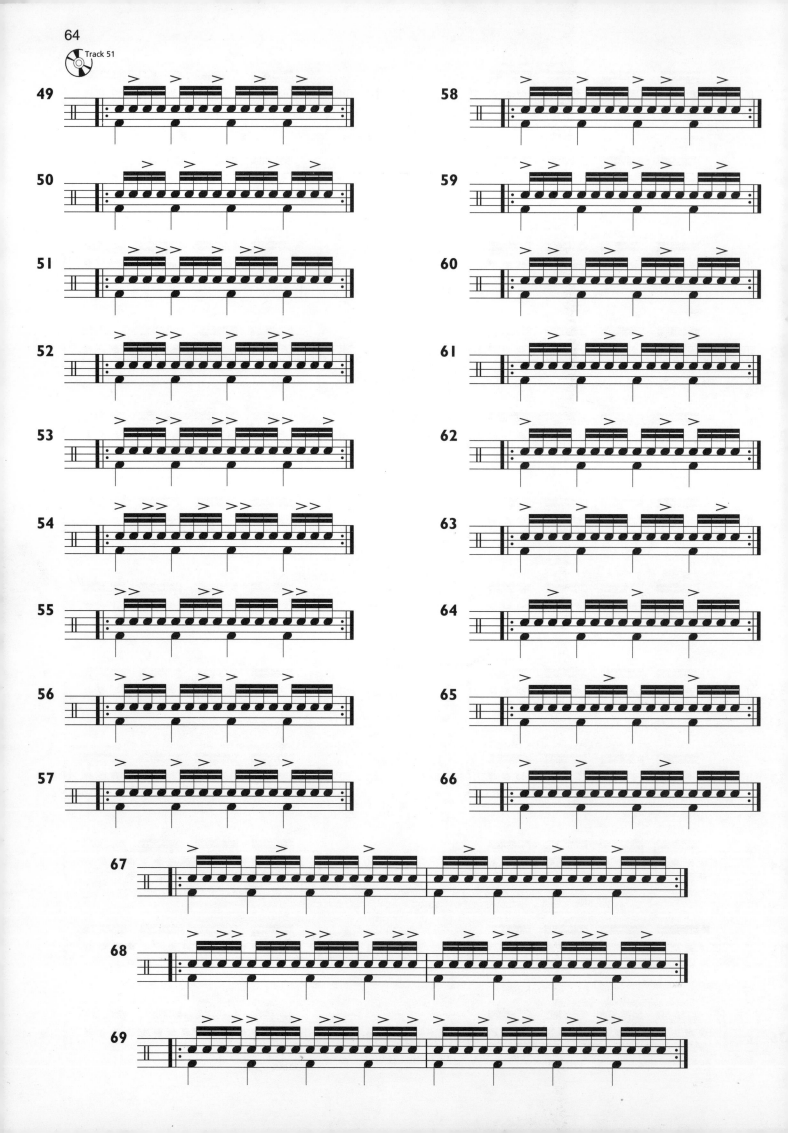